Tucker's Tracks

A Speech/Language Book on Interactive Play with Up & Down Concepts

eler

Let's Connect! Visit simplicityhappens.com and subscribe to receive adorable language and cognitive development activities for children ages 2-6!

Independently Published by Steph Winkeler

For permission requests contact: simplicityhappens@gmail.com

Published in the United States of America

ISBN: 9798372998391

For Little Ones

Every child I work with has helped me develop my tracks as a Speech-Language Therapist. I'll continue to learn and grow along with those I get the amazing opportunity to work with, and I'll continue along this wonderful journey with the wisdom to know there is always more to learn.

Thank you for teaching me the art of simplicity.

One step at a time.

Note from the Author

This story is dedicated to little ones. I have learned so much from my own children and the children I work with, and I continue to learn and grow with every step I take in this profession as a Speech-Language Therapist.

In *Tucker's Tracks*, your little ones will engage in an interactive adventure as they learn about the concepts (up & down) while following Tucker, an adorable bear, as he tracks from place to place throughout his day.

Tucker's Tracks is meant to create a positive and encouraging dialogue between parent/caregiver/educator and child in the following ways:

- *Tucker's Tracks* is designed for little ones, especially children ages 18 months to 5+ years old, and includes an interactive story dialogue, story vocabulary, and up & down concepts. Supplemental tracking sheets included for use as your child develops and grows their receptive and expressive knowledge of these skills.

- When the story gives the prompt, "Point to the bear," give your child time to listen, look for, and locate the intended picture target. Once your child identifies the intended picture target (e.g., pointing, labeling, responding) independently or with your support, continue with the story and respond by adding more language dialogue for your child to hear. The textual framework is there to help guide you through this interactive dialogue with your little ones.

- Look for the password to download the bonus activity so your little ones can use the movable Tucker bear to play along with the story. Fun background sheets are also included within the bonus activity to make up your own story (look for the password in this book to unlock the bonus activity).

I sincerely hope *Tucker's Tracks* invites dialogue, discussions about bear habits, and up & down concepts. Best of all, I hope using the movable Tucker bear helps your child learn while playing as there is no better way to build speech & language skills! As always, wishing you memorable reading moments with your little ones!

Sincerely,

Steph Winkeler

P.S. Don't forget to look for the secret password to unlock more *Tucker's Tracks* activities!

Table of Contents

Tucker Bear walks up the hill.
He walks up, up, up.

Tucker feels hungry.
He sees berries.
Mmm, Mmm, Mmm!

What is Tucker doing?
He is eating the berries.
Chomp, Chomp, Chomp!

Tucker is all done eating.
He goes down, down, down.

What is Tucker doing?
He is swimming.
Swish, Swish, Swish!

Tucker swims up, up, up.
Splash, splash, splash!

Here comes a fish.
Fish swims up, up, up.
Bubble, Bubble, Bubble!

Oh-no!
Tucker catches the fish.
Will he eat the fish?

No! Tucker lets fish go.
Fish swims down, down, down.
Hurry, Hurry, Hurry!

Tucker walks up the mountain.
He walks up, up, up.

What is Tucker doing?
He is climbing the tree.
He climbs up, up, up.

It starts to snow. *Oh-no!*
Tucker climbs down the tree.
He goes down, down, down.

Tucker walks in the snow.
The snowflakes go down, down, down.
Sprinkle! Sprinkle! Sprinkle!

Tucker walks down the mountain.
He goes down, down, down.
Tucker feels cold.
Brr, Brr, Brr!

Tucker feels tired.
He sees a warm den.
Snuggle, Snuggle, Snuggle!

What is Tucker doing?
He is sleeping.
Shh, Shh, Shh!

He sleeps in the cozy den during the cold winter months.
Zzz, Zzz, Zzz.

NOTES

Looking for the movable Tucker Bear?
Visit **simplicityhappens.com** and click on
Speech and Language Books>**Tucker's
Tracks**> and type in this password:

Tuckerbear!

Tucker's Tracks: Vocabulary Concepts

berries

Tucker

fish

snowflakes

tree

den

18

Vocabulary Concepts: Receptive Tracking Sheet

Ask your child, "Where is the...(snow)?" Place a check mark in the box next to the vocabulary words that your child <u>receptively</u> identifies (e.g., pointing) within the story or on the picture vocabulary page (p. 20).

Where is the...?

| snow | ☐ |

Where is the...?

| tree | ☐ |

Where is...?

| Tucker | ☐ |

| den | ☐ |

| fish | ☐ |

Where are the...?

| berries | ☐ |

Notes

_____
_____
_____
_____
_____
_____
_____
_____

Picture Vocabulary

Vocabulary Concepts: Expressive Tracking Sheet

Point to a picture and ask your child, "What is this?" and "Who is this?" Place a check mark in the box next to the vocabulary words that your child <u>expressively</u> states within the story or on the picture vocabulary page (p. 22).

What is this…?

snow	☐

What is this…?

a tree	☐

Who is this…?

Tucker	☐

a den	☐

a fish	☐

What are these…?

berries	☐

Notes

_____

_____

_____

_____

_____

_____

_____

Picture Vocabulary

Up & Down Concepts: Tracking Sheet

Place a check mark in the box next to the concepts that your child identifies on p. 24 (e.g., "Show me where Tucker is going *up* the hill."). Once your child identifies the concepts receptively (e.g., pointing), ask them to tell you what is happening within each picture (e.g., see "Expressive" below). To give your child support, say "Is Tucker walking *up* or *down* the hill in this picture?"

<u>Receptive</u> ☐	<u>Expressive</u> ☐
Show me where Tucker is swimming in the water? (d)	Point to the picture and say, "Tell me what Tucker is doing in this picture?" (d)
<u>Receptive</u> ☐	<u>Expressive</u> ☐
Show me where Tucker is walking up the hill? (c)	Point to the picture and say, "Tell me what Tucker is doing in this picture?" (c)
<u>Receptive</u> ☐	<u>Expressive</u> ☐
Show me where Tucker is eating berries? (a)	Point to the picture and say, "Tell me what Tucker is doing in this picture?" (a)
<u>Receptive</u> ☐	<u>Expressive</u> ☐
Show me where Tucker is walking down the hill? (b)	Point to the picture and say, "Tell me what Tucker is doing in this picture?" (b)

Up & Down

Up & Down Concepts: Tracking Sheet

Place a check mark in the box next to the concepts that your child identifies on p. 26 (e.g., "Show me where Tucker is going *up* the hill."). Once your child identifies the concepts receptively (e.g., pointing), ask them to tell you what is happening within each picture (e.g., see "Expressive" below). To give your child support, say "Is Tucker walking *up* or *down* the hill in this picture?"

Receptive ☐	Expressive ☐
Show me where Tucker is walking down the hill? (c)	Point to the picture and say, "Tell me what Tucker is doing in this picture?" (c)
Receptive ☐	Expressive ☐
Show me where Tucker is climbing in the tree? (b)	Point to the picture and say, "Tell me what Tucker is doing in this picture?" (b)
Receptive ☐	Expressive ☐
Show me where Tucker is walking up the hill? (a)	Point to the picture and say, "Tell me what Tucker is doing in this picture?" (a)
Receptive ☐	Expressive ☐
Show me where Tucker is sleeping in the den? (d)	Point to the picture and say, "Tell me what Tucker is doing in this picture?" (d)

Up & Down

a

b

c

d

Check Out the following Speech/Language Books by Steph Winkeler
Use the QR Codes (next to cover photo) or search for the books on Amazon!

Go on an adventure with Bruno, an energetic puppy who chases his favorite red ball from his yard to the park and back home again. Create a fun and exciting dialogue with your little ones when you ask,

"Where is Bruno's Ball?"

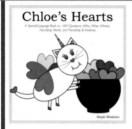 

Join Chloe, a compassionate unicorn cat, on her travels as she learns how the simple act of sharing creates the magic of kindness & kinship. Support your child's understanding of Who, What, & Where Questions, Color Knowledge, and Describing Words when you share the magical story of Chloe's Hearts with your little ones!

Help Addy, an adventurous little girl, discover the magical crown, map, and cape to harness her superpowers and find the buried treasure on the island of *Cool Cove* while learning story vocabulary words with initial /k/ & /g/ sounds.

Follow Hattie, Ziggy, and Pixie, three hard-working honeybees, as they set out together to search for flowers and collect nectar for making delicious, golden honey! Create teachable moments with your little ones when you give the directions to,

"Point to the first bee."
"Point to the bee in the middle."
"Point to the last bee."

Your LITTLE ones will love being BIG helpers as they guide Teddy, a determined gingerbread cookie, on finding his way home. Go on a BIG & LITTLE learning adventure together when you read *Teddy's Travels* with your little ones.

This book is perfect for the fall and winter seasons with lovable characters and delicious candy along the way.

Sully, the snowman, enjoys playing in the cold outdoors, but what will happen to Sully when the big bright sun appears in the sky?

Your little ones will enjoy responding to each question with yes or no while learning about the concept of negation as they spot Sully and his friends playing outside.

Made in the USA
Monee, IL
15 February 2023

27898306R00021